Upon Awaiting Redemption

Special Edition

A Collection of Poetry

By James D. Richards

Upon Awaiting Redemption

Special Edition

Reflection of Poetry

By James D. Richards

Cadmus Publishing
CadmusPublishing.com

Upon Awaiting Redemption: Special Edition Manufactured in the United States of America. Copyright 2025 by James D. Richards All rights reserved. No part of this book may be reproduced in any form, audio, digital, or in print, except excerpts by reviewers, without written permission from the copyright holder or Cadmus Publishing LLC.

DISCLAIMER:
 The thoughts, opinions, and expressions herein are those of the author and do not reflect those of Cadmus Publishing LLC. Any similarities to actual events or people are purely coincidental. Names and distinguishing characteristics may have been changed to preserve the identities of any individuals. Published by Cadmus Publishing LLC. P. O. Box 8664. Haledon, NJ 07538

Web: Cadmuspublishing.com
Facebook.com/Cadmuspublishing
Business email: admin@cadmuspublishing.com

ISBN# 978-1-63751-531-0

Book Catalog Info Categories:
 Poetry

Cadmus Publishing
CadmusPublishing.com

Special Thanks To
Diane and the Humans of San Quentin team Giving a voice to the unheard
humansofsanquentin.com

TO THE READER

Greetings, I would like to thank all of you who read the first edition of Upon Awaiting Redemption. Your letters of support and your donations were encouraging and greatly appreciated. You have let me know that my writings are serving their intended purpose of reaching your hearts and inspiring you to inspire others. At the request of many of you that read the first edition, I have decided to expand the descriptions and details of my poems to include the specific origins of inspiration. I am happy to honor your requests by allowing you to view or envision specific sources of my inspiration. In addition, you will find that I have included several new poems and writings that I hope you will enjoy.

For those of you who have not read the first edition of Upon Awaiting Redemption, I would like to share with you a brief glimpse into my past so that although your experience of my writings will be uniquely yours, you may perceive the origin of my inspiration through knowing some of my past experiences.

I grew up on the southeast side of Fresno California. I was raised in a household with both my parents, along with two beautiful and loving sisters. My family's financial status could be classified as middle class; we didn't have a lot of money, but we weren't poor. My father worked and my mother stayed home with us kids and ran a small daycare. Outside the walls of my house, I grew up around drug dealers, pimps, gangsters, and killers-the likes of Which were not only unavoidable but embraced with love and devotion, as some were of the same bloodline as myself.

At the same time, there were several people in my life who were wise, intelligent, religious, and belonged to the so-called higher class of society. I was fortunate to attend a performing arts middle school as well as a performing arts high school. I was trained in musical theater, visual arts, studio production, musical instruments, vocals and more. At the age of ten I was part of a group of child performers that performed as opening act for plays at dinner theater. Some of the plays actually starred Broadway sensation Audra McDonald when she was a teen, I would ask her to sing every time I saw her.

A constant and consistent dominant factor in my life, even as a young boy, was a loving attraction I felt toward the intrinsic nature of women. By the time I was in my mid-to-late twenties I had been intimately involved with hundreds of women. Don't take it the wrong way, I'm not bragging or boasting I'm giving you the accurate truth so that you can follow the steps of what you will find that came to be.

My life took a turn in 1996 when, at the age of 19, I joined the military. I was stationed in San Diego, CA, but the military lifestyle wasn't for me. A buddy of mine who was also serving got kicked out and moved in with his older prostitute girlfriend in a shady motel on the "hoe stroll" where I would visit them frequently. One day my buddy's girlfriend told me that some of the girls were asking her about me. I was not overly impressed until she explained that they were prostitutes looking for a pimp. I had no firsthand experience in that game but I was naturally intrigued. She schooled me on what to say if one of them approached me. Sure enough, a few days later I was approached by three of them at the same time. Two asked me what they would have to do to be with me, before I could answer, the third, more experienced than the other two, reached into her bra and pulled out about five hundred dollars and gave it to me with the words, "I choose you." She turned to the other two and told them they would have to do the same thing. Just like that, I was in the game.

We travelled from city to city for a few weeks, even though I didn't really know what I was doing, but I was making money and that's all that mattered to me. That endeavor ended with all of us getting arrested in Orange County. It turned out that one of the young ladies was underage, so I went jail and was sentenced to probation even though I was unaware that she was under age.

Unfortunately, that incident did not discourage me enough to the point of quitting the lifestyle. When the internet started poppin' in the early 2000's, the sophistication level went up and so did the money. For a long time I was having it my way-nice cars, nice house, big money, entertainment companies, all things which to me at the time reflected success. When I try to recall the number of women that choose me in the game I come up with thirty-something.

There are some whom perceive the nature of my exploits as luster, or unique status of prestige, I assure you that it is not. The game did something to my heart, my mind, and my soul that is not easily described, though perhaps you may find understanding within the writings you are about to read.

Over the years I developed a very bad habit at the blackjack table. I remember sitting at the tables betting six hundred dollars a hand, winning five thousand one night, losing ten thousand the next. Up-Down-Round and Round, as quick as I would make money in the game is as quick as I would lose it at the tables.

My life went on like that for about 15 years, accumulative of tales resembling fantasy and fiction, but it was my reality. My addiction to blackjack, coupled with all of the other aspects that came with the lifestyle I was living, drove me to the brink of insanity. I was tired of going in circles and ready to give up. I decided to break it off with the woman that was with me at the time and for us to go our separate ways, but she did not want to go and she did not want me to leave. I will never forget the look on her face as I attempted to make my exit. She stood in front of the doorway blocking me from leaving with a sword in her hands. Her arms were outstretched, pointing the sword toward me. *As* I tried to reach around her for the door knob, the sword entered my flesh.

Obviously I survived, but a piece of me did die that day, it pushed me over the edge. For a brief while I believe I actually did go insane. I was messing up real bad, doing things totally out of my normal character. In the middle of all that, both my parents got sick at the same time. My father had a massive stroke, and while he was recovering, my mother was diagnosed with breast cancer. I left the remnants of what was once everything to me behind and moved in with my parents to provide them care; that was 2011. I was mad at the world and everything in it. My actions during that period of time in my life landed me where I am today and where I have been for the last thirteen years, in prison, wrongfully convicted of sexual assaulting two self-admitted prostitutes, sentenced to life. I am diligently fighting to regain my freedom.

Upon awaiting redemption, I often reminisce; these are the thoughts and words that come to mind...

"When a person comes to the realization that what they have falsely perceived as their own success or achievement came at the cost of the surrendered virtues and relinquished morality of others, the self-reflection necessary for true atonement weighs heavy." See for yourself...

See For Yourself

Sometimes I get so frustrated, aggravated,

Because my mistakes though few and far in between are aggregated.

What seems real ain't always true.

But you hear it so much that it's real to you.

Make believe and fabrication,

Blinded and binded through manipulation.

Borrow my eyes and see what I see,

Then look in the mirror and see if you see me,

Or is it just me, looking at you,

Saying what seems real ain't always true.

Who do you trust, what do you believe?

You can look through my eyes but you aren't me.

You must be everything or nothing at all.

You must stand firm and never fall.

You must be a stone, you don't ever cry.

You must think you're brave because you aren't afraid to die.

You must like risk; you take so many chances.

You must be something to look at, you get so many glances.

You must be a user, all the people that you use.

You must be stupid, you don't win more than you lose.

You must be guilty, look at all the signs.

You must be crazy, looks like you lost your mind...

But I am none of that, I don't think that's me.

Now I need my eyes back, for myself I have to see.

Trust Issues

I have trust issues. I find it hard to trust

For I know men that for next to nothing will leave you in the dust.

My trust in you will weaken me I'm skeptical of your intentions.

I don't feel right, I'm paranoid, my name too much is mentioned.

The wall is comfort, I lean against it not having to watch my back,

But even the wall built by man is vulnerable to collapse.

To know me well is complicated, I'll keep you at a distance.

The closer you get the further I'll go, pursuit will meet resistance.

My frame of mind, the way I am, can't be the only way,

But until I change the words "trust me" is the worst thing you could say-

James D. Richards *Upon Awaiting Redemption: Special Edition*

Three Lonely Friends

I told you I have trust issues,

That is why I have few friends.

I guess I wish that I had more,

But I guess it really depends.

Me I say that I don't care,

The fewer friends the better.

Me I say I could care less,

If the time it takes is never.

Myself I created this emptiness,

Perhaps with encouragement from others.

Myself I negate possibilities,

Possibilities are silently smothered.

But I say I have three friends,

That I may call loneliness a lie.

The three friends I say I have

Are Me, Myself and I.

Better Than Myself

No more mistakes or misinterpretations,
Just rewards and congratulations.
Hesitation not confused with procrastination,
It takes time to look at what I'm facin'.
Slow my role on the dice be patient,
Hasty in my way wishing I would have waited
For the right time dedicate it to my loved ones
So elated, tell my future self I finally made it,
Look at what God created let me reiterate it...
I'm better than myself.

"Let not your days be rewound to times of blunder and foul, your future is much more bright than your past may allow."

Win This Fight

Trying to find my inner self

At times I do feel lost.

The cost my faith depends on me

At times I do feel crossed.

On the other hand, on the flip side,

I feel like I know why.

My sins created a knot of karma

Not easy to untie.

I tell myself its not my call,

God is the one who will judge us all.

Damn I hope I'm right,

That all the lessons that I learned

Make me victorious in this fight.

James D. Richards   *Upon Awaiting Redemption: Special Edition*

Chasing Losses

Double or nothing means do it again

Try your luck, try not to bust,

First mind instinct don't hesitate come up.

Think of the possibilities,

Instantaneous stability.

All in one shot.

Take what they give or give what you got.

Feel the rush but don't get crushed.

Double or nothing means do it again,

But you already lost, and you might not win.

Humble's Lesson

On top of the game by means of no shame.

But your ass got knocked in the grass.

Soiled by the earth;

No humility in your stability,

But bounce back from your loss.

Just another road to cross.

Get up and be meek,

The ground you're on belongs beneath your feet.

A Sound Choice

How much more deaf are you than a man born deaf? If you choose not to hear, how much more deaf are you than he? If you choose not to hear the argument of your adversary, if you pay no attention to words that you hear, if you make no attempt to gain understanding, if your actions reflect those of one who cares not of wrong occurrence if the wrong is not against he, though others suffer. Even a man born deaf is able to make a sound choice, so may you.

Reach Teach Preach

Situational poetry flows as essential elements,
Theorize criticize humanize classify
Open eyes mesmerize fortify,
Teach.
Ghetto streets suburbs lofts city suites,
Reach.
Minds imprisoned captured by propaganda.
Too blatant to be recognized as subliminal,
Candy coated resistance logged as minimal.
Minds searching for truth misled,
Minds taught that fish and bread keep the poor man fed,
Preach.
Words of truth to solicit youth,
Tell them to be aware of bags offered under flag of truce.
That those believed in never stop earning trust,
That the wrong choice could mean ashes to dust.
Beautiful words read or heard,
Use them to reach, use them to teach,
And when called upon, use them to preach.

Dollars And Sense

For the majority of my life I entertained the pursuit of riches. Dedicated, persistent, and committed to a never ending paper chase. In finding my niche, paper was accumulated as easy as the guarantee that a man's sinful lust will possess him to spend foolishly on a woman. As easy as I obtained my so-called riches; more easily did I let them slip away. Easy come easy go, a fool and his money will not have a long-lasting relationship. So disrespectful was I, in gain and in loss. However, in chasing my riches, I would often in moments of sanity accrue priceless wealth. Much more appreciated and respected was the wealth I acquired, mainly from those who had come many years before me. So if you are out there chasing paper, I'll be the first to tell you, "Getcho money," and I wish you all the luck in accumulating wealth.

Cherish Value and Worth

There are many of whom which I placed value upon, monetary value, what they were worth to me. A tragic misfortune, you see, the value I placed upon the many was not equivalent to their worth. I exploited their value instead of cherishing worth- I know now that their worth would have brought more than the value I placed upon them but because I did not cherish their worth, their value depleted; soon after they were dismissed, no longer needed. Cold way to be, in my heart it truly hurt- I valued them with such regard, but I did not cherish their worth.

"I do not think that I have ever truly been in love, perhaps once when I was sixteen, perhaps. But the thought of being in love, being truly in love as I have never experienced, mystifies me. Though it eludes me, I write much of love."

Lonely Hearts Desire

To those whom seek but yet have not acquired,
Of what unknown, heard nor shown,
A lonely heart's desire.
Hands can't touch, lips can't feel,
Fabricated substance, though it seems real.
You dream of love heart open and hand,
But what you seek cannot be planned.
No guarantee it will find you twice,
So when you find your heart's desire,
Hold on to it for life.

James D. Richards *Upon Awaiting Redemption: Special Edition*

Beautiful Flower

Picked for unique beauty offered as a show of affection.
Persuasively seductive flattering recipients,
Gaining favor for the one who ironically caused her demise.
Well enough to be left in placed connected to that which gave life.
If only she was not as she is but will soon not be.
For she was picked for unique beauty
Offered as a show of affection.
Comforted only by the joy her short thereafter life will bring.

Time Does Not Exist

I look at you like a star ever shining,
Time does not exist in your love.
You are everything, you are forever if only forever were more,
For time does not exist in you love.
No word in the language of your love to express doubt.
No method of measurement in attempt of wonder:
For measure, has no meaning, only how love speaks to love.
A beautiful mystery only two understand.
A love that will always be if only always were more,
For time does not exist in your love.

Thoughts of You

You are beautiful.

Though your beauty is not common it is unique and precious.

What more of beauty can be said than that which you reflect.

A gem of priceless value quantified only by its owner's desire.

Let no man understand the beauty I see in you.

Indescribable

We use the most beautiful words in our language to describe the most beautiful things, but words fall short or simply do not exist to accurately tell the story of your beauty. My hesitance in your description is complementary. I can speak of the color of your eyes, the texture of your hair, your smile, your skin, your shape, but your beauty is indescribable.

"I remember once, a beautiful woman stood before me blushing at the way I looked at her. She said; 'why are you looking at me in such a way?' I replied, 'I wasn't looking at you, I was looking in you."

You And I Together

I was not surprised to find myself mesmerized
By your lips your eyes
Your hips your thighs
Though I realized the reality of the situation,
There could be no compromise.
Trickeration
Not at my convenience to authorize.
So I mention from the gate,
And hope you can relate,
A decision to be made
And baby time don't wait.
Not selling dreams of cream,
We will really get it.
By yourself you are blessed
With me you are uplifted.

Together Strong

Its not for better or for worse,
Placement of position
You will always be first.
How could you stand in front of me
And not be in my way.
How could you stand beside me
And let come what may.
Instead reside in the elements of one,
Beside in the relevance of what will become.
Looking at your future gotta put on glasses.
Lavish ravish, see it gotta have it.
Want it you got it, no one can stop it.
Be right there make sure you don't drop it.
All I have is yours, as long as you are with me.
And I will never forget what it took for you to get me.

Once

She loved me once.
Once she loved me.
Her eyes were open but could not see,
She loved me once she belonged to me.
I did not love her back or even treat her right.
Once she loved me, she did not love me twice.

"Many years ago I met a beautiful young woman named Jackie in Bakersfield California. After spending time with her on a couple of occasions when I was passing through, she took me to meet her parents. I thought to myself, this girl must have the wrong impression."

Wrong Impression

She noticed that I noticed her,
I think she got the wrong impression.
I could tell she was interested,
But I think she got the wrong impression
Intrigued with the alternative to her current reality,
Her mind portrayed fantasy of finally living lavishly.
I want to approach her, I know she wants the same thing.
I hope she understands what wasted time brings.
She just wants to get to know me,
I think she got the wrong impression.
I want to get to know her,
But I think she got the wrong impression.
I know that if I go in she may never want to leave,
But imma tell her when to stop, when to go, imma tell her when to breathe.
She's acting hella giddy, ready to be infatuated,
Show me to her people so she can be congratulated.
She noticed that I noticed her
But I think she got the wrong impression.
She's going to end up with her feelings hurt,
Because I think she got the wrong impression.

Manipulated Love

Where does a man learn to love a woman? Is it something that can be taught? Is it possible that a man learns to love a woman from the way his father loves his mother? Is a mother's unconditional love for her son, or lack thereof, the foundation upon which a man's knowledge of love is built? Wherever or however a man learns to love a woman, it is imperative that he also learns the ways in which not to love.

For many years I viewed love as an art form, a special technique or tool used for the purpose of manipulation. I looked deep into her eyes as if searching for the origin of her soul, hypnotizing, her heart eager with anticipation, her mind confused by overwhelming emotion, her body at a heightened sensitivity to touch... At that perfect moment I said to her, "The only way to express through words the way I feel for you right now is to tell you the truth, and the truth is, 'I love you.' " A lie told with such ease as though the definition of the word was nonexistent. I lied about loving her only to be loved in returned. You see, I wanted her to love me because I define to her what love is, because if she loves in the way which I define, there is nothing she will not do for me...

Then along came Sarah Shine. *As* the many before her, I looked into her eyes and told her that I loved her. She looked back at me with disbelief and disgust, and said, " There is no need to lie, I will do as you please." She laughed and said, " You and my ex would have made a great team, he could control with his fists, as he does, and you could tell them you love them to console them, as you do."

I was silenced by shock, but laughing inside. You see, she respected my time and appreciated my knowledge and concern, but most of all, she despised the way I manipulated love.

Emotionless

I feel emotionless
The way you are looking in my eyes,
I don't want to make you cry,
Make you die inside.
Alive with no soul
I did not think possible,
Until I emerged from what should have been your essence,
You were hallow.
I should have pulled out sooner,
Before it was an empty place.
I should have looked away sooner,
Before you were all up in my face,
But I felt emotionless,
So it was easy to disregard the fact
That I may have destroyed a part of you
That you may never get back.
Wish I could have drank a potion
So I could have felt devotion,
But I felt emotionless,
Unless feeling emotionless is an emotion.

" It is an unfortunate reality that the majority of the females that chose me in the game experienced sexual abuse during their childhood. Perhaps moreso that their vulnerabilities were exploited. They are the inspiration for She Looks To Me, and A Daughter's Father."

She Looks To Me

The depth of her moral affection is shallow, near empty. Once full allotted by a tender promise when wondrous amaze awaited exploration. Drained by her abusers replaced with confusion of love, what love is supposed to be. Now in front of me with hopes of replenishment from being drained by a tender promise of love, of what love is supposed to be,
she looks to me.

A Daughter's Father

She doesn't understand how much he cares,
She cannot comprehend, ashamed and unaware.
She barely speaks she holds her tongue dazed and confused.
Her head held down her mouth scared shut from fear of another bruise.
He cocks his hand she covers her face,
He tells her to sit she knows her place.
She cooks she cleans and continues to love,
Devoted and loyal she will not budge.
Shattered as she is hard to put together,
You open your arms and try to make it better.
Your eyes from tears are red,
Your neck is stiff but you turn your head.
A cry for help she does not bother,
But what if she was your daughter, or he was your father.

Ancient Teardrop

Things of the past which my eyes have seen but my soul could not comprehend until now.
Recognizing the evil not from a perspective of moral and emotional integrity, rather, from a perspective of confused conflict.
Things such as, when deciphered later in life, cause emotional instability and psychological vulnerability where an average man's sanity is easily reversed.
Suppression is a false comfort hidden in darkness yet recognizable to the empathetic.
Anger, vengeance and spite, praying to release.
Then, I did not cry holding on to tears clenched in anger. Now, I pray, ancient tear drop.

Precious Soul

Precious soul of the pure light, shine pure.
Held between two hands from top and bottom not seeming to touch.
Connected by rays from the north, south, east and west, shine pure.
No words, no resist, submissive without thought to whom from which you began to whom from which you begin.
Precious soul of the pure light.

Contact this author at: James D. Richards #AS6943
Ironwood State Prison C1-110 Po Box 2199 Blythe CA
92226

"Do something good or change something bad."

Time don't miss me
Let me tell you bout time...
Time required
Time design
Time desired
Time be kind
Time be mine
Time take a chance
Time never end
Time understand
Time reveal
Time heal
Time be patient
Time just don't be wasted

Bout Time

In the time it takes for time to pass you by
Time in the blink of an eye
For when your eyes close time still thrives
When they open again
Time is no more than when it begins I don't know if
time is my enemy I'm not sure if time is my friend
If time never stops shall I never end
Time soothe me
Time move me
Time don't lose me
Time use me
Time hold up
Time wait
Time don't be late
Time diminish my fears
Time soak my tears
Time correct me
Time don't reject me
Time select me
Time don't forget me
Time I'm ready
Time be with me

There Is Beauty

Beauty is much more than what we see. Imagine you do not have the privilege of sight, that you cannot see what others perceive as beautiful. A look described as beauty is that which is appealing to the eye often derived from social influence. However, when it is discovered, what beauty can offer, you will find that there is beauty in a touch, there is beauty in passion, there is beauty in words, there is beauty in struggle, there is beauty in what you have accomplished, there is beauty in most everything you do with pure intentions. The world is beautiful by much more than what we see.

Super Kid

I'm eight years old, fearless and bold, there is not much that scares me,
So I grab dad's pack when he's asleep, okay this is kind of scary.
I go to the bathroom I lock the door I'm at the toilet bowl,
I take a cigarette between my finger and thumb and slowly begin to roll.
Rolling back and forth butt facing up this is my favorite game,
The stuff falls out into the water I smile I have no shame.
I roll and roll one by one until they all are empty,
The more he buys and tries to hide the more and more he tempts me.
I'm eight years old but I'm not dumb I want my dad to live,
So I play my game that's what I do, I'm just a little kid.

"It is amazing the capacity of understanding that a child may possess. When I was a child my father became very ill and was told by his doctor that he must stop smoking. I went into super kid mode."

Misplaced Dreams

He comes to steal your dreams, although so real it seems,
The night goes by, you open your eyes but don't remember a thing.
Beautiful thoughts, fantastic adventures,
The world was yours and all its splendor.
Low and crude foul and rude it was not his to take,
The day goes by to your surprise there's been a big mistake.
You find your dream tucked away or simply just misplaced.
Sleep tight my friend and worry not, your dreams he cannot take.

Playful Hearts

Playful hearts dance carefree, ceaselessly smiling basking in the spirit of infinite joy. Single moments divided only by echoes of euphoria now held instantly in the present. Constant, unsullied, and without intention, innate ignorance of that which would otherwise taint immaculacy. Twirling and circling connected by grasp counter-balanced by steadiness. Perfect, not confined to parameters of situational convenience but always. Without definition or explanation, assurance unnecessary however definite. Unprepared to conclude or thereafter for the infinite joy of now is all.

Just Enough

I have enough because I have God,
Because I have God I have enough.
No more no less than what He provides,
Enough is defined in each sunrise.
No wrong in prosper, success or achievement,
When He and I are in agreement.
What more can He give than everything?
What more than His Son can sacrifice mean?
Joyful, happy, and thankful,
Though loss to the heart is painful.
For what it is worth we all must learn
That what we have lost is of no concern.
I have enough because I have God.
Because I have God I have enough.

Back Seat Driver

I'm a back seat driver, turn here turn there, speed up slow down. I'm looking out for both of us, keeping in mind the intended destination, but I feel like you're not listening and I hate being ignored. Why are you not going the way I want you to go? The driver speaks, "You better calm down before I pull over and let you out! You can walk, and I'll drive right along the side of you, watching you stumble, watching you trip and fall. I'll get out and help you up, and let you continue to walk. I'll watch as your feet blister and care for your wounds. I'll watch the weather fall upon your head, and when your legs give out, I will carry you. Is that what you want? See, I'll get you where you need to be, but this is my ride, my hands are on the wheel, my foot on the gas, and the route is mapped."
I humbled myself and said, "Lets roll."

Loyalty

Priceless is loyalty. True loyalty, not false or that which can be bartered or bought, that which is craved by kings and longed for by queens. True loyalty is insulted when defined as friendship, even love cannot compare. It is the willingness of death, to live for and to die for that which you are loyal to, or to whom you have pledged loyalty, not to a point, but absolute. Be loyal to yourself, be loyal to God, beyond that I will not advise, for your loyalty may bring great success if you are wise, or it may very well lead to your demise.

Necessity, Faith, And Worth

As directed by faith, a man pushes a large boulder, larger than he, up a mountain. More than tedious the struggle, the weight hard to bear, he continues step by step, push by push. He turns and rests the boulder at his back and contemplates, Necessity, Faith, and Worth.

James D. Richards *Upon Awaiting Redemption: Special Edition*

Guardian Angel

I met an angel today, I asked if I could borrow his wings.
He explained that the cost for his wings was far beyond the realm of imagination,
far beyond that which can occupy space or be perceived by senses.
No material thing, no matter the exquisite tangibility can compare.
I was not asking to have them, just to use them for a short while.
I stood strong and undeterred in my persistence, I could not be turned away
angel tell me of things beyond my understanding I will listen to what you say.
There was a soft and joyful laughter in his smile as he covered me with his wings.
He said, " I cannot give you my wings, for I know not what you'll do, but though they were given to me, these wings were meant for you."

You Are Brave

You lift your voice to speak against wrong even when others don't
You stand and fight, no fear or flight, even when others won't
You seek no praise, your passion leads, righteous are your intentions
Adversaries tense, position in defense, when your name is mentioned
For those who doubt do not for long, as they count your many victories
Dare not oppose fearing defeat forever remains in history
When you're long gone, many things will be said in many different ways
But when they speak your name I know they'll say, Forever you were brave

www.ingramcontent.com/pod-product-compliance
Lightning Source LLC
Chambersburg PA
CBHW052149070526
44585CB00017B/2047